Lessons on Demand P

Teacher Guide and Novel Unit for Scythe

By:

John Pennington

The lessons on demand series is designed to provide ready to use resources for novel study. In this book you will find key vocabulary, student organizer pages, and assessments.

This guide is divided into two sections. Section one is the teacher section which consists of vocabulary and activities. Section two holds all of the student pages, including assessments and graphic organizers.

Now available! Student Workbooks!

Find them on Amazon.com

Section One

Teacher Pages

Vocabulary

Suggested Activities

Part 1 and 2 Vocabulary

Remorse

Foreboding

Patron

Sycophant

Enmity

Pariah

Austerity

Antithesis

Dubious

Malfeasance

Enigmatic

Esoteric

Part 1 and 2 Activities

<u>Reading Check Question / Quiz:</u>

What color is a Scythe not suppose to wear? Black

Who does Scythe Faraday take as his apprentices? Citra Terranova and Rowan Dim-Damisch

What is a group of Scythes called? An Elegy

What stipulation does the Scythedom set for Scythe Faraday's apprentices? The one chosen to become a Scythe must glean the other.

<u>Blooms Higher Order Question:</u>

Critique each of the 10 Scythe commandments.

<u>Suggested Activity Sheets (see Section Two):</u>

Character Sketch—Citra Terranova

Character Sketch—Rowan Damisch

Character Sketch—Faraday

Character Sketch—Ben Terranova

Character Sketch—Tyger Salazar

Research Connection—St. Louis

Research Connection—Artificial Intelligence

Draw the Scene

Who, What, When, Where and How

Part 3 Vocabulary

Sardonic

Penance

Mantra

Charisma

Revelry

Epiphany

Effigy

Platitude

Infamy

Stoic

Audacity

Repertoire

Part 3 Activities

Reading Check Question / Quiz:

Who is Citra's new instructor? Scythe Curie

Who is Rowan's new instructor? Scythe Goddard

Why is Esme important? She is the Xenocrates daughter

When does Citra fall under the jurisdiction of the Thunderhead? When she is being revived

Blooms Higher Order Question:

Appraise the actions of six characters and determine if they are moral, support your decision.

Suggested Activity Sheets (see Section Two):

Character Sketch—Goddard

Character Sketch—Curie

Character Sketch—Xenocrates

Character Sketch—Esme

Research Connection—Falling Water

Research Connection—Neuron

Precognition Sheet

What Would You Do?

Part 4 and 5 Vocabulary

Perpetuity

Algorithm

Indignation

Resonance

Claustrophobic

Staunch

Rouse

Inauguration

Empathy

Threnody

Requiem

Dirge

Part 4 and 5 Activities

Reading Check Question / Quiz:

Who is Gerald Van Der Gans? Faraday

What does Citra disguise herself as to avoid getting captured? A toniest

Which of Goddard's disciples is not killed by Rowan? Volta

Who is ordained at the Winter Conclave? Citra/Anastasia

Blooms Higher Order Question:

Defend a stance on the Scythedom is it necessary or should it be abolished? Provide a minimum of three supporting statements.

Suggested Activity Sheets (see Section Two):

Character Sketch—Volta

Character Sketch—Rand

Character Sketch—Chomsky

Character Sketch—Possuelo

Research Connection—Prometheus

Research Connection—Anastasia Romanov

Create the Test

Interview

Top Ten List—Events

Write a Letter

Chapter Vocabulary

Chapter Activities

Reading Check Question / Quiz:

Blooms Higher Order Question:

Suggested Activity Sheets (see Section Two):

Discussion Questions

Section Two

Student Work Pages

Work Pages

Graphic Organizers

Assessments

Activity Descriptions

Advertisement—Select an item from the text and have the students use text clues to draw an advertisement about that item.

Chapter to Poem—Students select 20 words from the text to write a five line poem with 3 words on each line.

Character Sketch—Students complete the information about a character using text clues.

Comic Strip— Students will create a visual representation of the chapter in a series of drawings.

Compare and Contrast—Select two items to make relationship connections with text support.

Create the Test—have the students use the text to create appropriate test questions.

Draw the Scene—students use text clues to draw a visual representation of the chapter.

Interview— Students design questions you would ask a character in the book and then write that characters response.

Lost Scene—Students use text clues to decide what would happen after a certain place in the story.

Making Connections—students use the text to find two items that are connected and label what kind of relationship connects them.

Precognition Sheet—students envision a character, think about what will happen next, and then determine what the result of that would be.

Activity Descriptions

Pyramid—Students use the text to arrange a series of items in an hierarchy format.

Research Connection—Students use an outside source to learn more about a topic in the text.

Sequencing—students will arrange events in the text in order given a specific context.

Support This! - Students use text to support a specific idea or concept.

Travel Brochure—Students use information in the text to create an informational text about the location

Top Ten List—Students create a list of items ranked from 1 to 10 with a specific theme.

Vocabulary Box—Students explore certain vocabulary words used in the text.

What Would You Do? - Students compare how characters in the text would react and compare that with how they personally would react.

Who, What, When, Where, and How—Students create a series of questions that begin with the following words that are connected to the text.

Write a Letter—Students write a letter to a character in the text.

Activity Descriptions (for scripts and poems)

Add a Character—Students will add a character that does not appear in the scene and create dialog and responses from other characters.

Costume Design—Students will design costumes that are appropriate to the characters in the scene and explain why they chose the design.

Props Needed— Students will make a list of props they believe are needed and justify their choices with text.

Soundtrack! - Students will create a sound track they believe fits the play and justify each song choice.

Stage Directions— Students will decide how the characters should move on, around, or off stage.

Poetry Analysis—Students will determine the plot, theme, setting, subject, tone and important words and phrases.

NAME:

TEACHER:

Date:

Advertisement: Draw an advertisement for the book

Chapter to Poem

Assignment: Select 20 words found in the chapter to create a poem where each line is 3 words long.

Title:

_____   _____   _____

_____   _____   _____

_____   _____   _____

_____   _____   _____

_____   _____   _____

NAME:

TEACHER:

Date:

Character Sketch

Name

Draw a picture

Personality/ Distinguishing marks

Connections to other characters

Important Actions

NAME:

TEACHER:

Date:

Comic Strip

Compare and Contrast

Venn Diagram

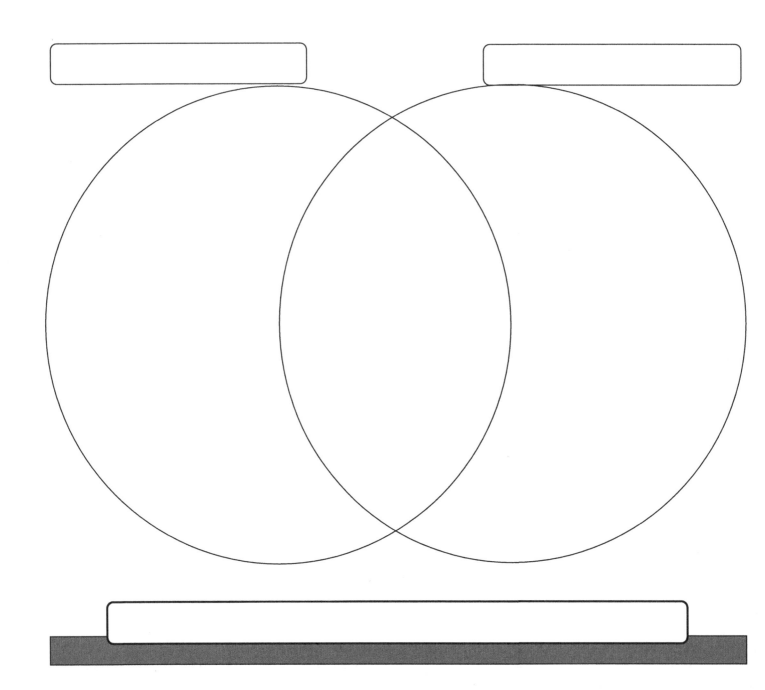

NAME:

TEACHER:

Date:

Create the Test

Question:

Answer:

Question:

Answer:

Question:

Answer:

Question:

Answer:

Draw the Scene: What five things have you included in the scene?

1   2   3

4   5

NAME:

TEACHER:

Date:

Interview: Who _____

Question:

Answer:

Question:

Answer:

Question:

Answer:

Question:

Answer:

Lost Scene: Write a scene that takes place between _____ and

_____

Making Connections

What is the connection?

NAME:

TEACHER:

Date:

Precognition Sheet

Who ?

What's going to happen?

What will be the result?

Who ?

What's going to happen?

What will be the result?

Who ?

What's going to happen?

What will be the result?

Who ?

What's going to happen?

What will be the result?

How many did you get correct?

NAME:

TEACHER:

Date:

Assignment: Pyramid

NAME:

TEACHER:

Date:

Research connections

Source (URL, Book, Magazine, Interview)

What am I researching?

Facts I found that could be useful or notes

1.

2.

3.

4.

5.

6.

NAME:

TEACHER:

Date:

Sequencing or timeline

1.

2.

3.

4.

5.

NAME:

TEACHER:

Date:

Support This!

Supporting text

What page?

Supporting text

What page?

Central idea or statement

Supporting text

What page?

Supporting text

What page?

NAME:

TEACHER:

Date:

Travel Brochure

Why should you visit?

What are you going to see?

Map

Special Events

Top Ten List

1.

2.

3.

4.

5.

6.

7.

8.

9.

10.

NAME:

TEACHER:

Date:

Vocabulary Box

Definition:

Draw:

Word:

Related words:

Use in a sentence:

Definition:

Draw:

Word:

Related words:

Use in a sentence:

NAME:

TEACHER:

Date:

What would you do?

Character: _____

What did they do?

Example from text:

What would you do?

Why would that be better?

Character: _____

What did they do?

Example from text:

What would you do?

Why would that be better?

Character: _____

What did they do?

Example from text:

What would you do?

Why would that be better?

NAME:

TEACHER:

Date:

Who, What, When, Where, and How

Who

What

Where

When

How

NAME:

TEACHER:

Date:

Write a letter

To:

From:

NAME:

TEACHER:

Date:

Assignment:

Add a Character

Who is the new character?

What reason does the new character have for being there?

Write a dialog between the new character and characters currently in the scene.

You dialog must be 6 lines or more, and can occur in the beginning, middle or end of the scene.

Costume Design

Draw a costume for one the characters in the scene.

Why do you believe this character should have a costume like this?

NAME:

TEACHER:

Date:

Props Needed

Prop:

What text from the scene supports this?

Prop:

What text from the scene supports this?

Prop:

What text from the scene supports this?

NAME:

TEACHER:

Date:

Soundtrack!

Song:

Why should this song be used?

Song:

Why should this song be used?

Song:

Why should this song be used?

NAME:

TEACHER:

Date:

Stage Directions

List who is moving, how they are moving and use text from the dialog to determine when they move.

Who:

How:

When:

Who:

How:

When:

Who:

How:

When:

Poetry Analysis

Date:

Name of Poem:

Subject:

Text Support:

Plot:

Text Support:

Theme:

Text Support:

Setting:

Text Support:

Tone:

Text Support:

Important Words and Phrases:

Why are these words and phrases important:

Made in the USA
Middletown, DE
16 June 2021